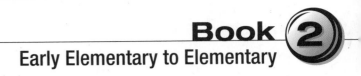

Famous & Fun Classics

13 Appealing Piano Arrangements

Carol Matz

Famous & Fun Classics, Book 2, is a wonderful introduction to the timeless masterworks of the great composers. The collection includes arrangements of themes from symphonic, operatic and keyboard literature, carefully selected for their appeal to younger students. The arrangements can be used as a supplement to any method. No eighth notes or dotted-quarter rhythms are used, and there are only easy departures from five-finger patterns. The optional duet parts for teacher or parent add to the fun of playing the arrangements. A section "About the Composers" can be found at the end of the book, which contains interesting biographical information in language that is easy to understand. Enjoy your experience with these musical masterpieces!

Alfred

Theme from
Fantasy-Impromptu

Frédéric Chopin (1810–1849)
Arr. by Carol Matz

DUET PART (Student plays one octave higher)

Romance

(from *Eine Kleine Nachtmusik,* 2nd movement)

Wolfgang Amadeus Mozart (1756–1791)
Arr. by Carol Matz

DUET PART (Student plays one octave higher)

The Merry Widow Waltz

Franz Lehár (1870–1948)
Arr. by Carol Matz

DUET PART (Student plays one octave higher)

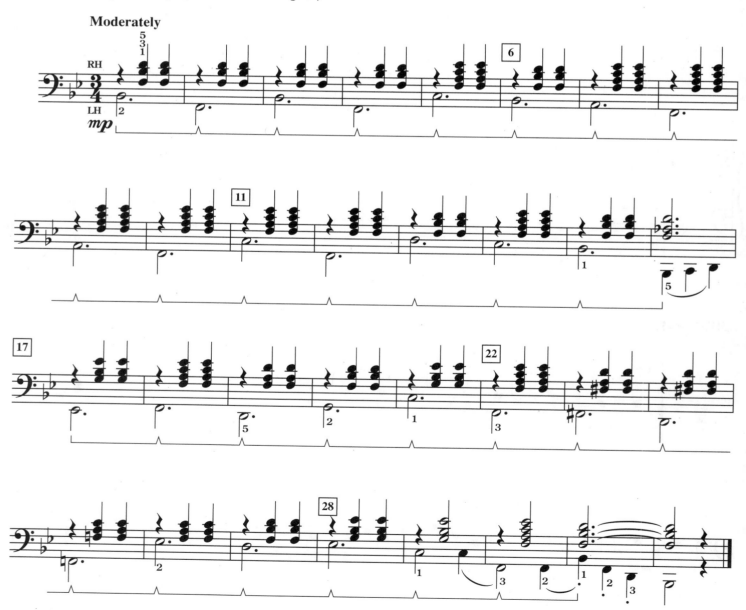

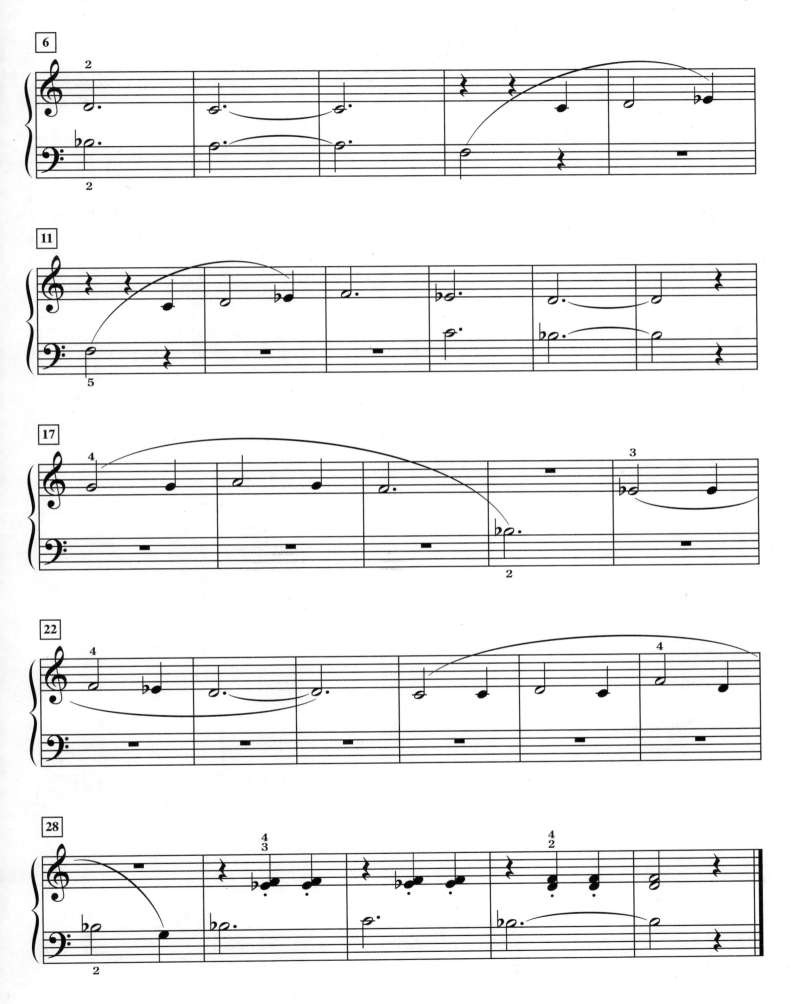

Pavane

Gabriel Fauré (1845–1924)
Arr. by Carol Matz

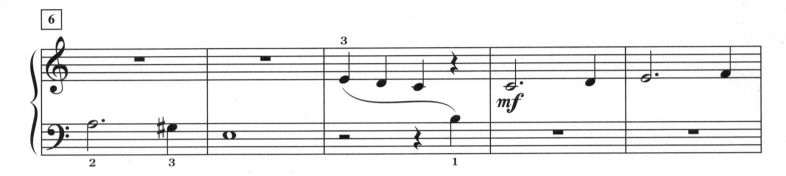

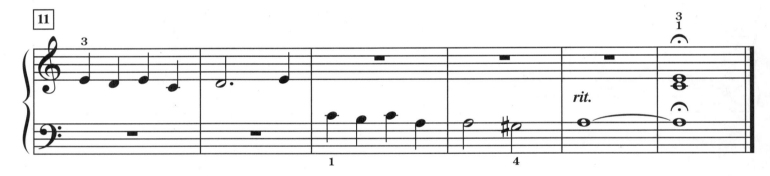

DUET PART (Student plays one octave higher)

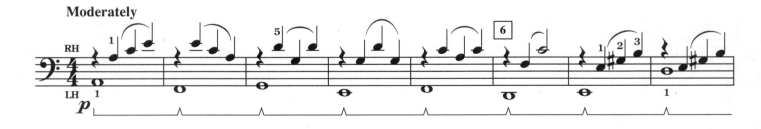

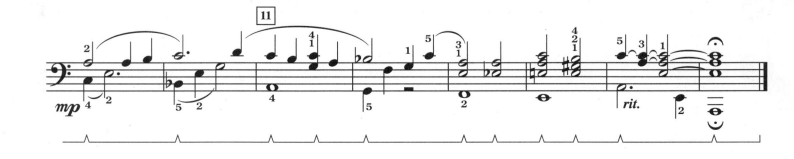

Nocturne

(in E-flat Major, Op. 9, No. 2)

Frédéric Chopin (1810–1849)
Arr. by Carol Matz

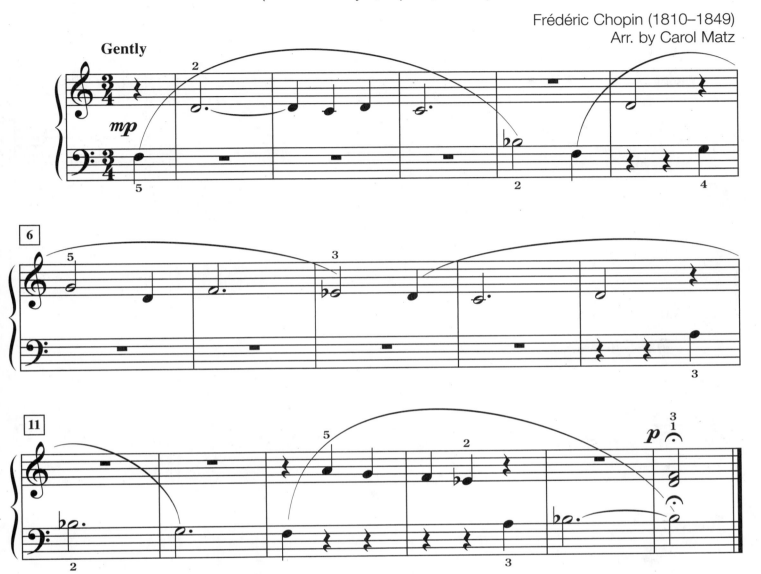

DUET PART (Student plays one octave higher)

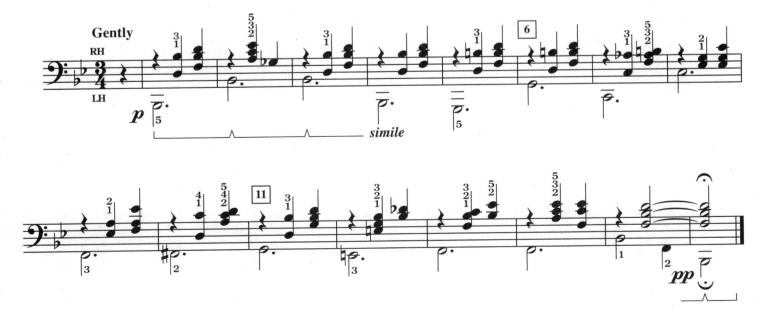

Can-Can

(from the operetta *Orpheus in the Underworld*)

Jacques Offenbach (1819–1880)
Arr. by Carol Matz

DUET PART (Student plays one octave higher)

Theme from Symphony No. 5

Peter Ilyich Tchaikovsky (1840–1893)
Arr. by Carol Matz

DUET PART (Student plays one octave higher)

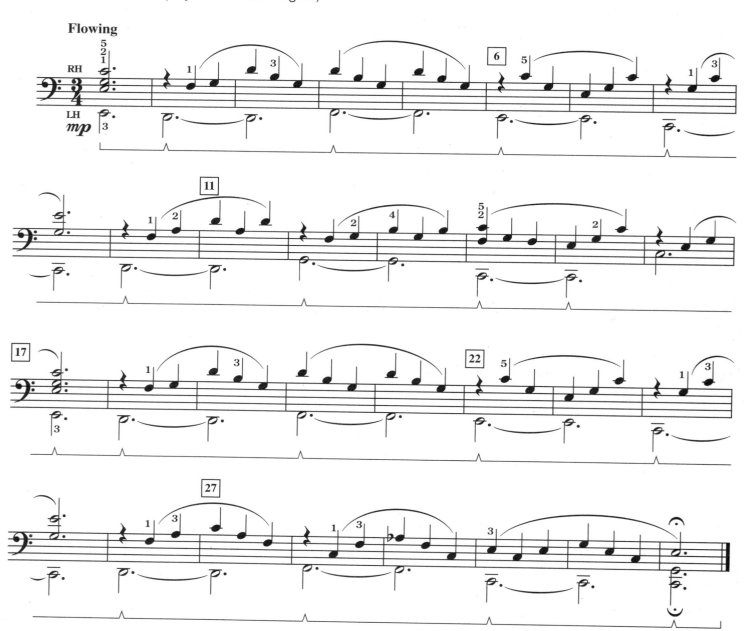

Rondeau

(from *Suite de Symphonies, No. 1*)

Jean-Joseph Mouret (1682–1738)
Arr. by Carol Matz

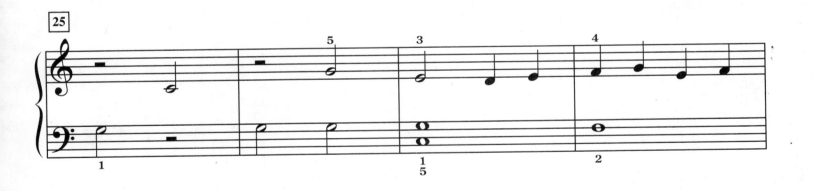

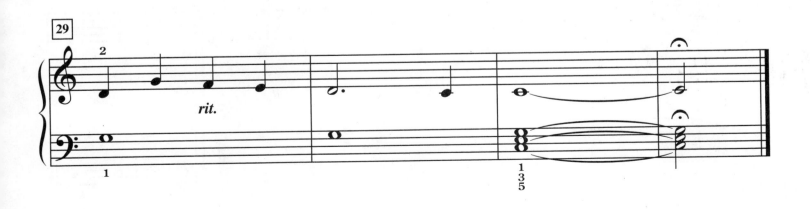

Egyptian Ballet Dance

(from the opera *Samson and Delilah*)

Camille Saint-Saëns (1835–1921)
Arr. by Carol Matz

DUET PART (Student plays one octave higher)

circle means move hand position

metro - 100 or 120

In the Hall of the Mountain King

(from *Peer Gynt Suite*)

Edvard Grieg (1843–1907)
Arr. by Carol Matz

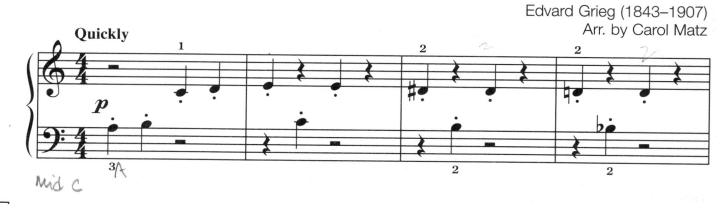

Mid C

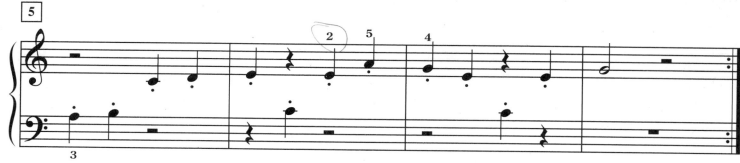

DUET PART (Student plays as written)

Jesu, Joy of Man's Desiring

Johann Sebastian Bach (1685–1750)
Arr. by Carol Matz

DUET PART (Student plays one octave higher)

Wild Horseman

(from *Album for the Young*)

Robert Schumann (1810–1856)
Arr. by Carol Matz

DUET PART (Student plays one octave higher)

Theme from the "Italian" Symphony

(Symphony No. 4)

Felix Mendelssohn (1809–1847)
Arr. by Carol Matz

Very fast and lively

DUET PART (Student plays one octave higher)

Very fast and lively

About the Composers

Johann Sebastian Bach
Born March 21, 1685; died July 28, 1750
Nationality: German

Bach was a great organist and church musician who composed all kinds of pieces for church services, keyboard instruments, orchestras and more. Besides his music, Bach is famous for having had 20 children! Four of his children grew up to become famous composers.

Frédéric Chopin
Born March 1, 1810; died October 17, 1849
Nationality: Polish

As a young child, Chopin was already composing and performing on the piano. When he was 20, Chopin left his home in Poland and moved to Paris, where he spent the rest of his life. Sadly, he was often ill and was only 39 when he died of tuberculosis. Chopin is remembered as one of the greatest composers of piano music.

Gabriel Fauré
Born May 12, 1845; died November 4, 1924
Nationality: French

Nicknamed "The Cat" by his friends, Fauré was very charming and made many friends during his life. He was an excellent pianist and organist, with a talent for improvising. At the age of 25, Fauré fought in the Franco-Prussian War and received a medal for bravery.

Edvard Grieg
Born June 15, 1843; died September 4, 1907
Nationality: Norwegian

Grieg grew up in Norway, and then moved to Germany to study music when he was a teenager. He became a wonderful pianist and gave concerts all over Europe, but every summer he went back to Norway to compose. Many of his pieces are based on the sounds of Norwegian folk music.

Franz Lehár
Born April 30, 1870; died October 24, 1948
Nationality: Austrian-Hungarian

Lehár received his first music lessons from his father, a horn player and military band leader. He studied violin and composition, and eventually joined his father's military band. He composed many waltzes and marches that became very popular in Vienna. His operetta *The Merry Widow* was his first big success.

Felix Mendelssohn

Born February 3, 1809; died November 4, 1847
Nationality: German

Mendelssohn's parents encouraged him to be a musician. The family regularly held afternoon concerts at their house, so Mendelssohn was surrounded by music at an early age. By the time he was a teenager, Mendelssohn had already written some of his greatest pieces.

Jean-Joseph Mouret

Born April 11, 1682; died December 20, 1738
Nationality: French

Mouret's father, a violinist, made sure that his son had the best musical training. Mouret became a very popular composer and held many important jobs. Later in life, however, he lost his jobs and his popularity. He ended up dying in a hospital for the mentally ill.

Wolfgang Amadeus Mozart

Born January 27, 1756; died December 5, 1791
Nationality: Austrian

By the time he was six years old, Mozart was an outstanding pianist, performing all across Europe. He composed his first piece of music when he was four, and wrote his first opera when he was twelve. Mozart wrote a huge amount of music and became a world-famous composer. Unfortunately, he died when he was only 35 years old.

Jacques Offenbach

Born June 20, 1819; died October 5, 1880
Nationality: German-born, lived in France

As a boy living in Germany, Offenbach was a wonderful cellist who gave public concerts. His father, a synagogue cantor, sent him to study cello in Paris, since he felt that Jews had more opportunities in France than in Germany. Offenbach became a successful theater conductor in France and composed about 90 operettas.

Camille Saint-Saëns

Born October 9, 1835; died December 16, 1921
Nationality: French

At the age of three, Saint-Saëns could already read and write, and began composing music. He eventually performed all over the world, traveling with his servant and his pet dogs. In his lifetime, Saint-Saëns composed more than 300 works and served as a church organist for over 20 years.

(continued)

About the Composers (continued)

Robert Schumann

Born June 8, 1810; died July 29, 1856
Nationality: German

As a young man, Schumann studied with a famous pianist whose star pupil was his daughter, Clara. Schumann fell madly in love with Clara (who became a famous pianist herself) and the two eventually married. A finger injury kept Schumann from becoming a concert pianist, so he became a composer. Clara gave the first performance of many of his piano pieces.

Peter Ilyich Tchaikovsky

Born May 7, 1840; died November 6, 1893
Nationality: Russian

Although Tchaikovsky began studying music as a young boy, he ended up going to law school and getting a job with the government. However, Tchaikovsky never lost his love of music and he eventually taught and composed music for a living. In 1891, he traveled to New York to conduct his music at the opening of the famous Carnegie Hall.